KALEIDOSCOPE

FOSSILS

by

Roy A. Gallant

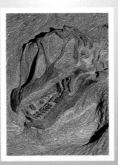

BENCHMARK BOOKS

MARSHALL CAVENDISH
NEW YORK

Series Consultant:
Christopher J. Schuberth
Division of Curriculum and Instruction
Armstrong State University

Benchmark Books
Marshall Cavendish Corporation
99 White Plains Road
Tarrytown, NY 10591
www.marshallcavendish.us

Library of Congress Cataloging-in-Publication Data

Gallant, Roy A.
Fossils / by Roy A. Gallant
p. cm. (Kaleidoscope)
Included bibliographical references and index.
Summary: Describes what fossils are, how they are formed,
and what they tell scientists about earth's past.
ISBN 0-7614-1041-4
1. Fossils—Juvenile literature. [1. Fossils. 2. Paleontology.] I. Title. II. Kaleidoscope (Tarrytown, NY)

QE714.5.G36   2000   560-dc21   99-047494

Photo research by Candlepants, Inc.
Cover photo: © Photo Researchers
Picture credits: © Photo Researchers: 5,6,9,13,14,17,18,21,25,27,28,31,32,35,36,39,40,43.
Diagram on page 10 by Gysela Pacheco. Map on page 22 by Jeannine L. Dickey.

Printed in Italy

CONTENTS

ABOUT FOSSILS

Fossils are the remains of animals and plants that lived very long ago. A fossil may form when an animal or plant dies and is quickly buried in mud or sand. A fossil may also form when marks left by an animal become buried. Over tens of thousands, or even millions of years, the mud or sand slowly turns to stone with the fossil locked inside.

By studying fossils, we can learn when and where the animal or plant lived and what the climate was like at the time. Fossils also tell us how life-forms have evolved, or changed,over thousands and millions of years.

Fossils, such as this Oreodon skull (a hog-like animal), some 35 million years old, are sometimes found just lying on the ground, exposed by wind and water. But such fossils are rare. Most remain buried and have to be carefully dug out of rock. This one was found in South Dakota.

6

WHAT ARE FOSSILS?

Many different kinds of animals and plants have lived on our planet for hundreds of millions of years before becoming extinct, or dying out. As some kinds have died out, others have taken their place. Among them have been dinosaurs, strange-looking shelled creatures called *trilobites*, and the ancestors of today's pine trees. We know a lot about Earth's past life-forms by studying fossils, and we keep learning more as new fossils are found.

Trilobites, like this one, swam through ancient seas for some 450 million years. They became extinct about 250 million years ago. They were hard-shelled animals, and were among the most successful of all prehistoric animals.

The word fossil comes from the Latin word fossilis, which means "dug up." Scientists who study fossils are called *paleontologists* (pa-lee-on-TALL-o-gists), a word from the Greek language that means "those who study ancient things."

Fossils may be an animal's footprint left in clay that later hardened into rock. Or fossils may be ancient worm borings or the teeth marks of large animals. They may be formed from an ancient tree trunk or animal bones. We even have fossil imprints of dinosaur skin. To qualify as a fossil, the animal or plant remains usually must be older than about 10,000 years.

Grasshoppers, ants, flies, and other small insects sometimes became trapped in the sticky pitch from ancient pine trees and so became fossils. The unfortunate grasshopper shown here met its sticky death some 40 million years ago in Kaliningrad, Russia.

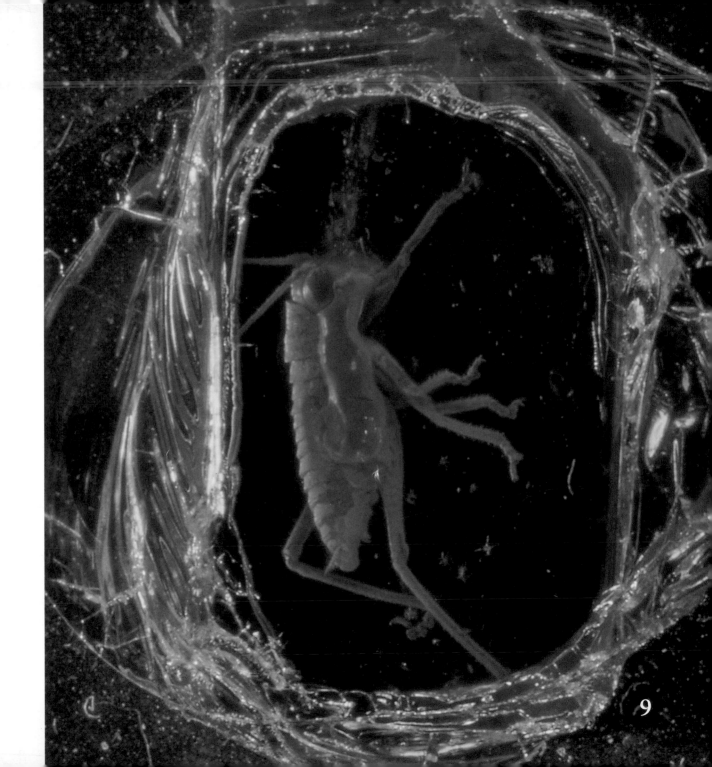

9

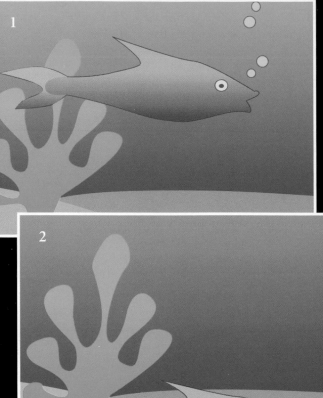

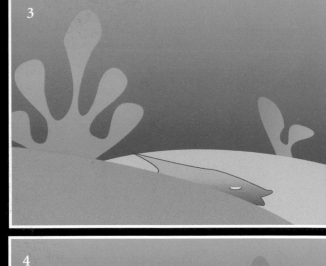

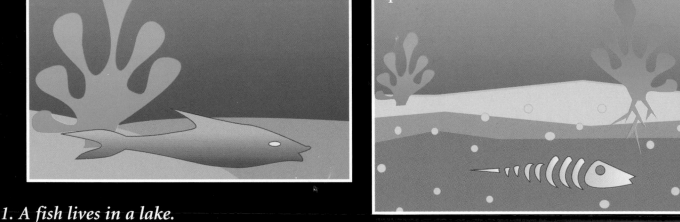

1. A fish lives in a lake.
2. The fish dies and sinks to the bottom of the lake.
3. The fish is buried in the lake-bottom sand.
4. The soft parts of the body decay, leaving only the bones. The bones sink deeper into the sand.
5. Millions of years later, the lake bottom sands hardens to rock and the fish bones or their imprint are preserved as a fossil.

HOW FOSSILS ARE MADE

To become a fossil, a plant or animal must first be buried in layers of soft sediments—mud, clay, or sand, soon after death. If it's not buried quickly, the hard parts—bone, shell, or wood, for example—can decay. Soft parts, such as skin and muscle, are rarely preserved. They usually decay too fast to leave fossil records. Finally, as the fossil develops it must not be disturbed too much. Over millions of years, the sediments are squeezed and hardened into sedimentary rock, along with the remains of the plant or animal. A fossil has been made.

Local climate plays a part, too. If it is very cold or dry, almost the entire animal may be preserved as a fossil. In Alaska and Siberia the remains of woolly mammoths have been frozen in almost perfect condition for more than ten thousand years. In certain dry caves in South America the fossil remains of huge animals called ground sloths have been almost perfectly preserved as mummies. But these cases are rare.

This baby mammoth fossil was found frozen in the ground in Russia.

13

The giant horned dinosaur called Triceratops stomped overland during the late Cretaceous period some 65 million years ago. This museum reconstruction was based on bones unearthed in Montana. The animal's actual bones were dissolved away but faithfully replaced by preserving minerals.

14

FROM BONE TO ROCK

You might be surprised to learn that a dinosaur skeleton in a museum is not made of the animal's original bones. Nature gradually made exact copies of the real bones. Here is what happened:

Water containing certain minerals slowly seeped into the ground and was soaked up by the bones. Slowly the mineral-rich water filled the tiny open spaces in the bones, making new "bones" that were even stronger and harder than the original. At the same time the bones gradually dissolved away.

Much later the pressure of the layers of sediment squeezed out the water, but the minerals, in the shape of the bones, were left behind. Such fossil bones are often very beautiful and colorful. Minerals such as quartz, calcite, or those tinted orange and red from iron have replaced the original bone material.

Different kinds of minerals can replace animal bones or tree remains and provide them with beautiful colors while preserving the bone or tree structure. This dinosaur bone fragment has been "agatized," meaning that minerals have turned the bone to agate, a type of rock.

This same process, called mineral replacement, also transforms shells and trees. Have you heard of petrified wood? Sometimes minerals replace the original living wood so perfectly that individual tree rings show up in full color millions of years later.

Mineral replacement has beautifully preserved these ancient tree trunks as "petrified wood." The actual wood was gradually dissolved away, but its structure has been preserved by minerals that replaced the wood. Such fossilized trees can be found in Petrified Forest National Park, Arizona.

Many fossils are only traces of past life—marks in stone. A dinosaur dies and its body sinks to the bottom of a swamp. The rough and leathery skin of the animal presses deep into the soft floor of the swamp. Over many centuries the skin dissolves away as the swamp mud turns to stone. Eventually, only an imprint of the skin pattern, called a mold, is left. Over hundreds of years, minerals collect in the mold and harden to stone. As they do, they take the exact shape and texture of the original dinosaur skin. In that way a cast is formed.

In western Canada fossil hunters have found casts made of sedimentary rock that show in sharp detail the skin texture of dinosaurs. Many casts of animal footprints have also been found.

Often imprints—or molds —of shells, footprints, and even dinosaur skin are found. This fossil shows what the hide of a Hadrosaur dinosaur looked like. Pour plaster of Paris into the mold and you produce a cast that can be painted to resemble the actual hide of the animal. This mold is some 65 million years old and was found in Mexico.

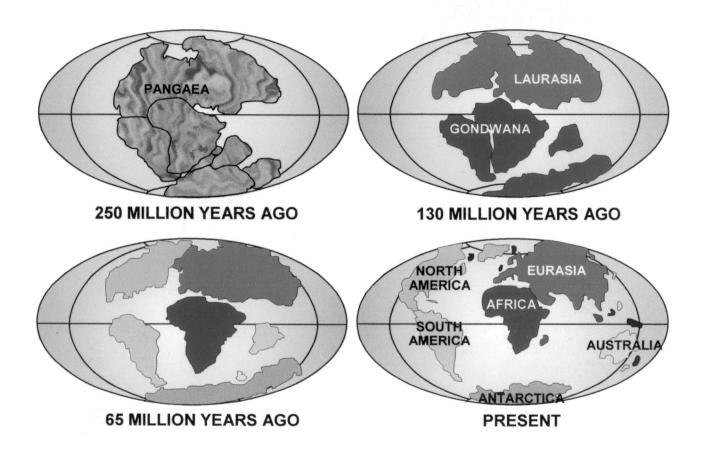

250 MILLION YEARS AGO

130 MILLION YEARS AGO

65 MILLION YEARS AGO

PRESENT

FOSSILS TELL US ABOUT EARTH'S PAST

Fossils tell us about animals and plants that lived long ago. And about changing climates and land forms, too. They are keys that unlock the secrets of Earth itself. They can show us that what is now a desert was once a forest and that what is now a mountain was once deep underwater. For example, if you find fossils of fish on a mountain, you know that what is now a tall peak was once underwater.

The changing face of Earth's surface through time. Some 250 million years ago there was an enormous supercontinent called Pangaea. By 130 million years ago, Pangaea had broken apart into the two lesser continents Laurasia and Gondwana. By about 65 million years ago, when the dinosaurs died out, the continents had further broken apart. Fossils have helped recreate the ever-changing puzzle of Earth's changing face.

What would you think if you found fossil tree ferns or magnolia plants beneath the ice sheets of Antarctica or Greenland? Scientists have found such warm-weather plants in both places. The fossils tell us that the climate of Greenland and Antarctica was much warmer millions of years ago.

It's hard to believe that this snow-covered land was once warm. But under the Greenland ice cap, scientists have found fossils of warm-weather plants, such as magnolias. Scientists can use fossils to discover what ancients climates were like in different parts of the world long ago.

24

When scientists cannot tell the exact date of a rock layer, they can turn to fossils for an answer. Over many years of studying fossils, scientists have learned that certain animal and plant groups lived before or after certain other groups. For instance, we know that, as a group, reptiles are older than mammals, amphibians are older than reptiles, and fishes are older than amphibians.

Each heavy line in the diagram represents a time of large-scale extinctions when thousands of species died out. At bottom, many animals lacking backbones died out some 440 million years ago. Higher up, many bony fish went extinct about 360 million years ago. Next, many amphibians and early reptiles, such as Dimetrodon, died out around 225 million years ago. Second from the top, early dinosaurs such as Stegosaurus went extinct about 190 million years ago. Top, T. rex and Triceratops died out near the end of the Cretaceous period some 65 million years ago.

So, say that we are curious about the ages of four different sedimentary rock layers in four different parts of the world. One layer has mammal fossils, another layer has reptile fossils, another has fishes, and the fourth layer has amphibians. Since we know which of those animal groups is oldest and youngest, we can say which rock layer is oldest or youngest, depending on the fossils it contains.

If you know how to look, and happen to be in the right place, you can read Earth's history in its rock layers, many of which contain fossils. These sedimentary rock layers in central Oregon expose hundreds of thousands of years of Earth's past.

For instance, a rock layer containing fossil bones of an ancient fish will be older than a rock layer containing fossils of mammals. And that is true of rock layers the world over. In this way, scientists can tell the relative age of rock layers.

What do these fish fossils tell us about the layer of rock they were found in?

31

Dinosaur bones are most often locked up in rock and are revealed by the careful chipping away of the surrounding rock. Visitors to Dinosaur National Monument in Utah can see where workers have exposed dinosaur bones by the thousands. It is one of the world's richest dinosaur bone graveyards.

THE TALES FOSSILS TELL

Paleontologists sometimes work like detectives. They collect all the clues they can and then try to figure out what happened. The following is a true story about an English paleontologist.

He was working in a stone quarry and found several large slabs of rock. Each slab had many fossilized pits made by raindrops 200 million years ago. By fitting the slabs together in their original position in the quarry, he could tell the direction of the wind that blew the rain that made the little pits. Not far from the quarry he found fossil footprints of several little animals. Some looked like miniature handprints with five fingers, one bent back.

The prints were puzzling because the "thumbs" were on the outside of the print, rather than the inside. A friend even suggested that the little animal might have walked cross-legged! But later the paleontologist realized that the fifth toe wasn't a thumb, but a shorter outside toe typical of many reptiles.

He also found the running footprints of an even smaller lizard-like animal. A careful study of the many prints told him what the larger animal was looking for—the smaller animal for dinner! From other rocks he learned about the plants that once grew in the quarry.

When a dinosaur bone is uncovered, workers carefully protect it from the air by applying certain chemicals. The bone fragment may then be wrapped protectively, carefully crated, and transported to the museum. There it will be further treated before being stored for researchers to examine.

Once safely in the hands of museum curators, a dinosaur fossil may be copied by pressing the bone into a soft material, making a mold. The mold is then filled with a material like plaster of Paris to make a cast of the bone. The cast is then painted to resemble the original fossil and put on display. Workers here are making a reconstruction of the largest meat-eating dinosaur ever found—Gigantosaurus. The 110-million-year-old giant was found in Argentina in 1993.

So by piecing together the fossil evidence, he was able to describe the environment of the quarry some 200 million years ago. He had a good idea of the kinds of plants and animals that lived there and what the weather was like. He concluded that the climate must have been mild, since reptiles could survive there. Reptiles are cold-blooded animals that need a warm climate to survive.

HUMAN FOSSILS—WHO WERE OUR ANCESTORS?

Since the 1800s, thousands of fossils of human ancestors have been collected from many parts of the world. Each year important new fossil finds add to our knowledge about our human evolution from ape-like creatures who lived some five million years ago.

Human fossil bones found in various parts of the world are gradually unfolding the history of our human ancestors, going back at least 4 million years. The human skull cap at left has been punctured by the teeth of a leopard, whose jaw bone rests just beneath the skull cap. Match the puncture holes with the two teeth.

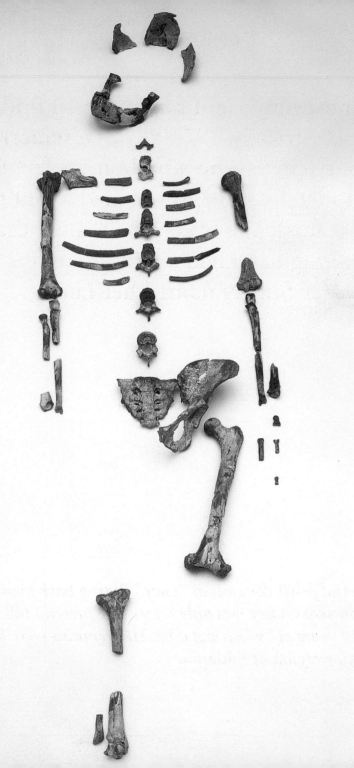

One of the most important human fossil finds was made in northeast Africa in 1974. It was a remarkable fossil skeleton of a female who stood only 3 feet 8 inches (112 centimeters) tall and weighed about 65 pounds (30 kilograms). She lived a little more than three million years ago and had a mixture of ape and human features. Her finders named her Lucy.

The partial fossil skeleton of "Lucy," dating back more than 3 million years. Lucy was only 4 feet (1.2 meters) tall and about 20 years old when she died. Her remains were found in the Afar region of Ethiopia.

Fossil footprints of a more recent human ancestor have been found in southern Africa. The prints are preserved in rock 117,000 years old. They were made by a lone figure walking across wet beach sand. Eventually time turned the sand to rock, and the footprints were preserved over many thousands of years. The prints are so detailed that they could have been made this morning. A young teenager today could step into the print and it would fit perfectly.

Thousands of fossils, such as these, are helping piece together the story of our human ancestors. That, surely, is the most exciting tale fossils can tell —the story of how human beings came to be on planet Earth.

Footprints back into the past lead anthropologists ever closer to answering the questions of when, where, and how human beings have evolved from creatures who lived as long ago as five million years. The footprint shown here has been preserved in volcanic ash.

43

GLOSSARY

Cast   Any substance, such as a mineral, that has hardened after filling a mold formed by a bone, for example, or some other animal or plant part.

Evolution   The changes over time in groups (species) of animals and plants. As changes in the environment —climate and temperature, for example—come and go, some species cannot stand the change and die out, or become extinct. New species then evolve and take their place.

Extinct   When an animal or plant species dies out, and no longer exists.

Fossil   The remains or imprints of animals or plants that have been preserved in rocks and are more than 10,000 years old.

Mineral   Any element (such as gold) or compound (such as quartz) found in nature that not alive and is the same wherever you find it.

Mineral replacement   The act of minerals dissolved in water seeping into a bone over the long time the bone is being turned into a fossil. Eventually, the bone dissolves away, the water evaporates, and what is left is an exact copy of the bone in the form or hardened minerals.

Mold   A hollow impression in a rock. The impression reveals the shape of a leaf, a shell or a footprint, for example, or some other part of an animal or a plant.

Paleontologist   A scientist who studies fossils.

Trilobites   Hard-shelled animals that became extinct about 250 million years ago.

FIND OUT MORE

Books:

Aliki. *Wild and Wooly Mammoths.* NY: Harper Collins Children's Books, 1995.

Craig, Janet. *Discovering Prehistoric Animals.* NJ: Troll Communications, 1990.

Giblin, James C. *Mystery of the Giant Bones: Digging Up the First Mastodon Skeleton.* NY: Harper Collins Children's Books, 1999.

Higginson, Mel. *Scientists Who Study Fossils.* NY: Rourke Corporation, 1994.

Patent, Dorothy H. *In Search of the Maiasaurs.* Frozen in Time Series. NY: Marshall Cavendish, 1998.

Tanner, Joey. Paleontology: *Dinosaurs and Other Fossils, Digging into the Past.* Learning Packets Science Series. AZ: Zephyr Press, 1993.

Websites:

Fossils! Behind the Scenes at the Museum:
www.rom.on.ca/quiz/fossil/

Fossil Zone:
www.discovery.com/exp/fossilzone/fossilzone.html

National Museum of Natural History (Smithsonian):
http://nmnhgoph.si.edu/

Science Magazines for Kids:
www.popmagazine.com
www.planetpals.com

Zoomdino.com:
www.enchantedlearning.com/subjects/dinosaurs/dinotopics.htm/

AUTHOR'S BIO

Roy A. Gallant, called "one of the deans of American science writers for children" by *School Library Journal,* is the author of more than eighty books on scientific subjects. Since 1979, he has been director of the Southworth Planetarium at the University of Southern Maine, where he holds an adjunct full professorship. He lives in Rangeley, Maine.

INDEX

Page numbers for illustrations are in boldface.